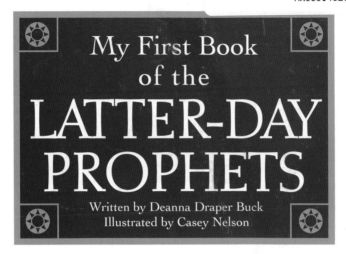

My First Book
of the
LATTER-DAY
PROPHETS

Written by Deanna Draper Buck
Illustrated by Casey Nelson

Nahia Darling

This book belongs to

Grandpa Larry and Nana Darling with much love!

Presented by

December 2017

Date

To my grandchildren

Elijah, Kjai, Meagan, Cirdan, Kiersten, and Mason

First printing in hardbound 2011
First printing in paperbound 2017

Library of Congress Cataloging-in-Publication Data
Buck, Deanna Draper.
   My first book of the latter-day prophets / retold by Deanna Draper Buck ; illustrated by Casey Nelson.
      p. cm.
   ISBN 978-1-60641-155-1 (board book)
   ISBN 978-1-62972-363-1 (paperbound)
1. The Church of Jesus Christ of Latter-day Saints — Presidents — Biography. 2. Prophets (Mormon theology) I. Nelson, Casey (Casey Shane), 1973–   II. Title.
   BX8693.B83 2011
   289.3'32092273 — dc22
[B]   2010011522

Printed in China   04/2017
RR Donnelley, Shenzhen, China

10   9   8   7   6   5   4   3   2   1

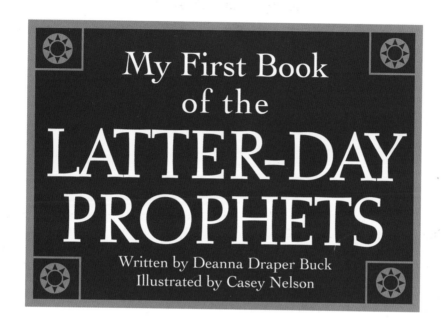

My First Book of the LATTER-DAY PROPHETS

Written by Deanna Draper Buck
Illustrated by Casey Nelson

DESERET
BOOK

SALT LAKE CITY, UTAH

PROPHETS

Heavenly Father has always talked with His people through His prophets. Prophets are men chosen by God who lead the Church and teach us about Heavenly Father and Jesus.

There were prophets long ago; we read about them in the Bible and in the Book of Mormon.

We have a prophet today who is the head of the Church on earth. The prophet listens to the Lord and receives messages from Him. From the time a prophet is a young boy, Heavenly Father guides and protects him so that when the time is right he will be prepared to lead the Church.

When we follow the prophet's teachings we are blessed.

JOSEPH SMITH, JR. (1830–1844)

Joseph Smith was the first prophet of the latter days. When Joseph was only seven years old, he needed an operation on his leg. The doctor didn't have any medicine to put Joseph to sleep or to stop the pain. Joseph told the doctor that he would be brave and stay still if his father would hold him during the operation.

After the painful operation, Joseph's leg got better, and he was eventually able to run and play, although he had a slight limp the rest of his life.

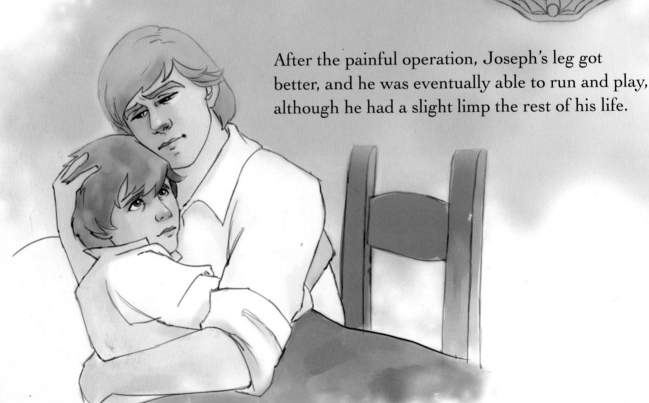

When Joseph was fourteen years old, he prayed to know which of all the churches he should join. In answer to his prayer, Heavenly Father and His Son, Jesus Christ, appeared to him in the Sacred Grove.

Later, with Heavenly Father's help, Joseph translated the Book of Mormon from the golden plates that had been placed in the Hill Cumorah by the angel Moroni. Through Jesus Christ, Joseph Smith organized The Church of Jesus Christ of Latter-day Saints.

As a prophet and the president of the Church, Joseph Smith sent out missionaries to preach the gospel, and the new converts helped to strengthen the Church. He directed the building of the Kirtland and Nauvoo temples. He received many revelations from Heavenly Father to instruct the Church, which are now in the Doctrine and Covenants. Joseph loved his family and took time to play with them and teach them, even though he was very busy.

BRIGHAM YOUNG (1844–1877)

Brigham Young's mother was sick most of the time when he was a boy, so he learned to make bread, churn butter, and prepare many of the family's meals by the time he was eight years old. Brigham learned how to work hard and take good care of the things he had.

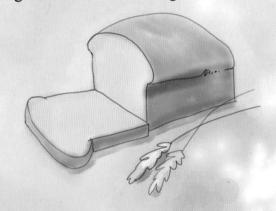

After missionaries taught him the gospel, Brigham Young wanted to meet Joseph Smith. As soon as he met him, Brigham knew that Joseph was a prophet of God. Brigham was always loyal to Joseph and was one of his trusted friends.

After the Prophet Joseph Smith was killed in Carthage Jail by enemies of the Church, Brigham Young was called by God to lead the Saints to the West, where they could get away from their enemies, build up the Church, and follow God's plan.

Brigham Young directed the building of the Salt Lake Temple. He asked some members of the Church to leave the Salt Lake Valley and settle in outlying areas—making new towns and building new farms and homes. Soon there were many towns, and the desert blossomed like a rose.

JOHN TAYLOR (1877–1887)

John Taylor was born in England. While he was young, his parents taught him to read the Bible and to pray. They also made sure that he had a good education.

When he grew up, he traveled to Canada, where he met Parley P. Pratt, who had been sent to Canada as a missionary. Elder Pratt taught John and his wife the gospel and baptized them.

John Taylor went with the Prophet Joseph Smith to Carthage Jail because he loved Joseph and wanted to help him. John had a beautiful voice and sang for Joseph and Joseph's brother Hyrum to comfort them while they were in jail.

When the angry mob killed the Prophet Joseph and Hyrum, John Taylor was shot several times. One bullet struck the watch John wore in his vest pocket. Even though he was badly hurt by other bullets, he was not killed.

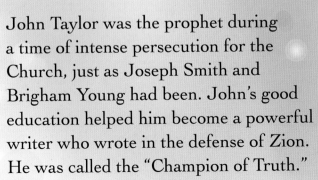

John Taylor was the prophet during a time of intense persecution for the Church, just as Joseph Smith and Brigham Young had been. John's good education helped him become a powerful writer who wrote in the defense of Zion. He was called the "Champion of Truth."

WILFORD WOODRUFF (1887–1898)

Wilford Woodruff had a lot of accidents when he was a child. He fell into a pot of boiling water, broke his arm, fell out of a tree, was kicked by an ox, and was chased by an angry bull. Wilford always felt as though Heavenly Father was protecting him because He had something important for him to do.

Wilford read the Bible while he was young, and he loved Heavenly Father. He was happy when he heard the missionaries teach, and he wanted to be a missionary too. While he was a missionary in England, he taught and baptized hundreds of people.

Wilford Woodruff was our prophet when the Salt Lake Temple was dedicated in 1893. He had been with Brigham Young more than forty years earlier when President Young selected the spot where the temple would be built.

Wilford Woodruff wrote in his journal every day for sixty-three years, recording important events in his own life and in the history of the Church.

LORENZO SNOW (1898–1901)

Both of Lorenzo Snow's grandfathers were
soldiers in the American Revolutionary War.
He liked to listen to them tell about fighting
for the freedom of their country. He thought
he would like to be a soldier too and serve his
country when he grew up.

After Lorenzo joined the Church, he
decided he would rather join the "Lord's
Army" and bring people to Christ. He
later went on five missions.

While Lorenzo Snow was our prophet, the Church did not have enough money to do all of the necessary things. There was a drought in Southern Utah, and President Snow promised the Saints there that the Lord would bless them with rain if they would pay their tithing.

They believed the Lord's promise and paid their tithing. The Lord did send rain, and their crops were saved. As the Saints throughout the Church continued to pay their tithing, the Church had enough money to continue its work.

JOSEPH F. SMITH (1901–1918)

Joseph F. Smith's father was Hyrum, the brother of the Prophet Joseph Smith. Five-year-old Joseph F. was very, very sad when he heard that his father and uncle had been killed in Carthage Jail.

Even though he was still a child, Joseph F. worked hard to help his widowed mother. He was eight years old when he drove the ox team for his mother as they crossed the plains to go to Utah.

Joseph F. was called on a mission to the Hawaiian Islands when he was only fifteen years old. It was a hard mission for someone so young, but he was a good missionary, and the Hawaiian people loved him.

While Joseph F. Smith was our prophet, some newspapers told lies and made fun of him and the Church. He always kindly and boldly defended the Church, and he didn't worry about what the newspapers said about him. He just did his best and left the rest to the Lord.

HEBER J. GRANT (1918–1945)

Heber J. Grant was shy as a young boy, but his mother always encouraged him to do his best. He wasn't a very good baseball player, so he practiced and practiced until he became good enough to play on a championship baseball team.

His handwriting was so bad that his friends made fun of it. He practiced until he had beautiful handwriting.

He couldn't sing well either, but after he took singing lessons and practiced a lot, he was able to sing a solo with the Mormon Tabernacle Choir.

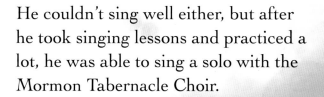

As our prophet, Heber J. Grant taught the Saints the importance of keeping the commandments, especially paying their tithing and keeping the Word of Wisdom. He also taught the Saints to work hard, and he promised them the Lord would bless them if they would do what was right.

GEORGE ALBERT SMITH (1945–1951)

As a young boy, George Albert Smith slept alone in an upstairs bedroom. When there was a storm and the wind blew hard, he would become frightened. He would get out of bed and pray that the house and his family would be safe. He knew that Heavenly Father heard his prayers, so he felt safe. Then he would get back into bed and fall peacefully asleep.

World War II was barely over when George Albert Smith was called to be the prophet. He went to visit Harry S. Truman, the president of the United States, and President Smith offered, on behalf of the Church, to send food, clothing, and blankets to the people of Europe, even those who had fought against the United States and the Allied nations during the war.

President Truman was surprised that the members of the Church wanted to help the people who had lost the war. President Smith told him that all people from all countries are children of Heavenly Father.

He said that the members of the Church wanted to show love and kindness to those in need. He hoped that everyone in the world would learn to love and help one another.

DAVID O. MCKAY (1951–1970)

David O. McKay was seven years old when his father was called on a mission to Scotland. While his father was gone, David became the man of the house and helped his mother milk the cows, feed the livestock, and do other work on their farm in Huntsville, Utah.

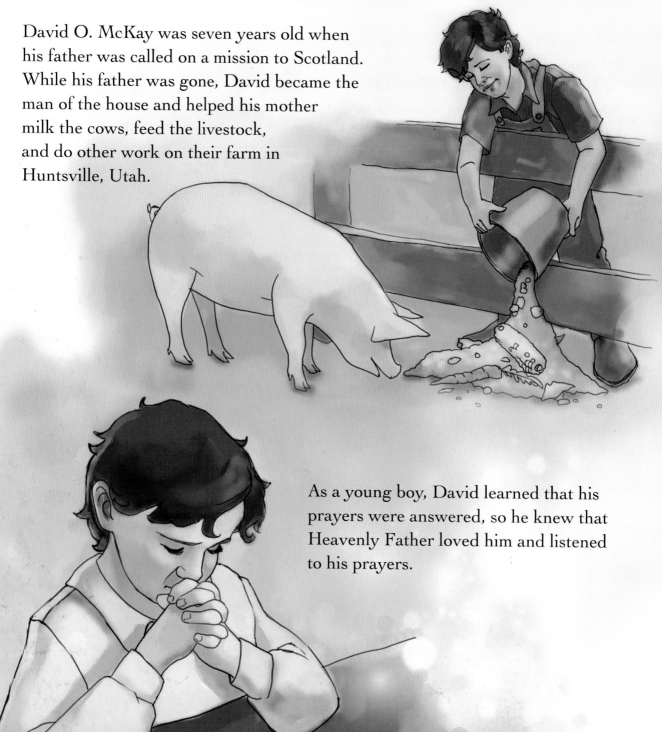

As a young boy, David learned that his prayers were answered, so he knew that Heavenly Father loved him and listened to his prayers.

As our prophet, David O. McKay taught that every member should be a missionary and be a good example to others. He taught parents that the most important work they would ever do would be in their own homes with their own families.

He loved all children. At one stake conference, he stayed after and shook the hand of every child who was there.

JOSEPH FIELDING SMITH (1970–1972)

Raised in Salt Lake City, Joseph Fielding Smith liked to play baseball and other games with his brothers, but most of all he liked to read.

In fact, he read the whole Book of Mormon two times before he was ordained a deacon.

Joseph Fielding Smith's father was the prophet Joseph F. Smith. Joseph Fielding is the only latter-day prophet whose father was also a president of the Church. Joseph Fielding liked history and served as Church historian for many years. He wrote many important books explaining the teachings of the Church.

He had a great love for his own family and for all children. As our prophet, he knew that people would become busier and busier. As his father had done, President Joseph Fielding Smith encouraged families to hold weekly family home evenings to help children learn the gospel and help children and parents love each other even more.

HAROLD B. LEE (1972–1973)

Harold B. Lee was raised in the small town of Clifton, Idaho. When he was a young boy, he saw some broken-down sheds in his neighbor's field. He thought it would be fun to explore the old buildings. As he started to climb the fence, he heard a voice telling him not to go there.

He stopped, looked around, and saw that he was alone. Then he knew that it was the voice of the Lord warning him of danger. Because he listened and obeyed, he was kept safe.

As our prophet, President Lee taught parents to teach their children to obey the commandments so that their families could be safe from the dangers of the world.

He urged parents to have family home evenings, to read the scriptures, and to have family prayer. He knew that doing these things would help us be better members of the Church and be safe and happy.

SPENCER W. KIMBALL (1973–1985)

Young Spencer W. Kimball set goals for himself.

When he was ten years old, he wanted to learn the words of the Church hymns by heart, so he sang the hymns to himself as he milked the cows on his family property in Thatcher, Arizona.

When he was fourteen years old, he heard a talk in church about reading the scriptures. He decided that he needed to read the Bible, and that very night he began reading it. Some of the Bible was hard for Spencer to understand, but a year later he was happy that he had met his goal to read the entire Bible.

As our prophet, Spencer W. Kimball taught the Saints to set goals. He asked us to "lengthen our stride."

Some of the things he asked us to do were to keep our yards and houses neat, plant gardens, keep a journal, learn another language, be better missionaries, and be good neighbors. He asked us to "do it now" and not wait until later.

EZRA TAFT BENSON (1985–1994)

Ezra Taft Benson grew up on a farm in Whitney, Idaho, and learned early on how to work hard. When he was five years old, he was already driving a team of horses and helping plow the fields.

When he was seven years old, his mother was the Relief Society president. He would help her harness the horses and get the buggy ready for her to go to her midweek Relief Society meeting. He would also load some wheat into the buggy for her to give to people in need.

When he was an Apostle, he was in charge of the disbursements of food and clothes to the people in Europe whose homes had been destroyed in World War II.

As our prophet, Ezra Taft Benson warned us against being prideful and urged us to read the Book of Mormon every day. He promised that we and our families would be blessed by Heavenly Father if we did.

HOWARD W. HUNTER (1994–1995)

Born in Boise, Idaho, Howard W. Hunter and his sister, Dorothy, were not baptized when they were eight years old. Their father, who was not a member of the Church, wanted them to wait until they were older. But Howard's mother taught him the gospel, and he gained a testimony of the Savior.

He fasted and prayed, and finally, when he was twelve years old and his sister was ten, their father said they could both be baptized. Later, their father was baptized too.

When Howard was forty-six years old, his father and mother went to the temple to be sealed. Imagine how happy Howard was to finally be sealed to his parents.

Howard W. Hunter was called to be our prophet when he was eighty-six years old. He served as the prophet for only nine months. In that short time, he taught us to be kinder to our families and neighbors. He also taught us the importance of being worthy to go to the temple and of making temple covenants with Heavenly Father.

GORDON B. HINCKLEY (1995–2008)

When Gordon B. Hinckley was a boy, he spent his summers on his family's small farm in the country, where he learned to work hard and to love the outdoors. During the school year, his family moved back to their home in Salt Lake City, where he loved to read the books in his family's large library.

As a new deacon, Gordon B. Hinckley attended a stake priesthood meeting with his father. As they sang the hymn "Praise to the Man," a song about Joseph Smith, Gordon received a testimony that Joseph Smith was a prophet of God.

While he was a missionary in England, Gordon became discouraged and thought maybe he should return home. His father told him to forget about himself and to work harder as a missionary. Gordon did as his father told him and became a good missionary.

When he was our prophet, President Hinckley taught us to go forward with faith, to do our best to live the commandments, and to be good examples to our friends. He loved the temple and caused many temples to be built around the world so that members could more easily go to the house of the Lord. He was always cheerful. He had faith that Heavenly Father is watching over all of us and His Church.

THOMAS S. MONSON (2008–)

Thomas S. Monson learned as a young boy to be thoughtful and kind to other people. His mother was a very good example to him. When poor men came to their house in the Salt Lake Valley and asked for food, she would always invite them in and give them a good meal.

As a boy, Thomas took Sunday dinner to a lonely neighbor every week.

When Thomas S. Monson was called to be a bishop, there were a lot of elderly widows in his ward. He visited them often and made sure that they knew they were loved and important to him and Heavenly Father.

President Monson likes to share stories of how living the gospel of Jesus Christ blesses us and others. He is very loving and always has a smile and a kind word for everyone.

Just like all the prophets before him, President Monson invites everyone, everywhere, to come unto Christ and enjoy the blessings of the restored gospel.

LATTER-DAY PROPHETS

Each of these prophets was different from the others, and each one brought special talents to his assignment. The revelations they received were needed by the Church and the world at that time.

JOSEPH SMITH, JR.
(1830–1844)

BRIGHAM YOUNG
(1844–1877)

JOSEPH F. SMITH
(1901–1918)

HEBER J. GRANT
(1918–1945)

GEORGE ALBERT SMITH
(1945–1951)

SPENCER W. KIMBALL
(1973–1985)

EZRA TAFT BENSON
(1985–1994)

HOWARD W. HUNTER
(1994–1995)

JOHN TAYLOR
(1877–1887)

WILFORD WOODRUFF
(1887–1898)

LORENZO SNOW
(1898–1901)

DAVID O. MCKAY
(1951–1970)

JOSEPH FIELDING SMITH
(1970–1972)

HAROLD B. LEE
(1972–1973)

GORDON B. HINCKLEY
(1995–2008)

THOMAS S. MONSON
(2008–)

Each was loved and respected by the members of the Church in his day, and we still honor each one today as a prophet of God.

About the Author

Award-winning, bestselling author Deanna Draper Buck and her husband have been married more than forty years. They currently live in Hooper, Utah, where she enjoys gardening, quilting, and entertaining their twenty-five grandchildren. Deanna has written thirteen LDS children's books, explaining gospel principles, Church history, and scripture stories in a simplified style.

About the Illustrator

Casey Nelson holds a degree in illustration and has worked as a figure drawing teacher in BYU's illustration department, performed in an improvisational comedy troupe, and been an artist for video games. After fourteen years working for the Walt Disney Company, Casey is now pursuing a master's degree in illustration and hopes to become a college professor.